GASTON
Goes to Mardi Gras

GASTON
Goes to Mardi Gras

Written and Illustrated by James Rice

The Illustrator of
CAJUN NIGHT BEFORE CHRISTMAS

FULL-COLOR EDITION

PELICAN PUBLISHING COMPANY
Gretna 2000

First printing, November 1977
Second printing, October 1983
Third printing, December 1987
Fourth printing, January 1995
Second edition, January 1998
Full-color edition, January 2000

The word "Pelican" and the depiction of a pelican are trademarks of Pelican Publishing Company, Inc., and are registered in the U.S. Patent and Trademark Office.

Library of Congress Cataloging-in-Publication Data

Rice, James, 1934-
    Gaston goes to Mardi Gras / written and illustrated by James Rice.
    — 2nd ed.
        p. cm.
    Summary: Gaston the alligator goes to New Orleans to celebrate Mardi Gras and joins in the "courir du Mardi Gras," watches floats being made, participates in the Zulu parade, and sees other typical sights.
    ISBN 1-56554-286-X (hc : alk. paper)
    1. Rice, James, 1934- 2. Alligators—Fiction. 3. Mardi Gras—Fiction.
4. New Orleans (La.)—Fiction. I. Title.
        PZ7.R3634Gat 1997
        [E]—dc21   97-3561
                                                                 CIP
                                                                 AC

Printed in Korea
Published by Pelican Publishing Company, Inc.
1000 Burmaster Street, Gretna, Louisiana 70053

GASTON GOES TO MARDI GRAS

One day while relaxing in the bayou, Gaston saw a poster announcing the Mardi Gras in New Orleans. He decided to go to the city.

On the way he joined a *Courir du Mardi Gras* group. They collected chickens and vegetables for the night's gumbo feast.

The gumbo feast was followed by a *fais-do-do* that lasted till dawn.

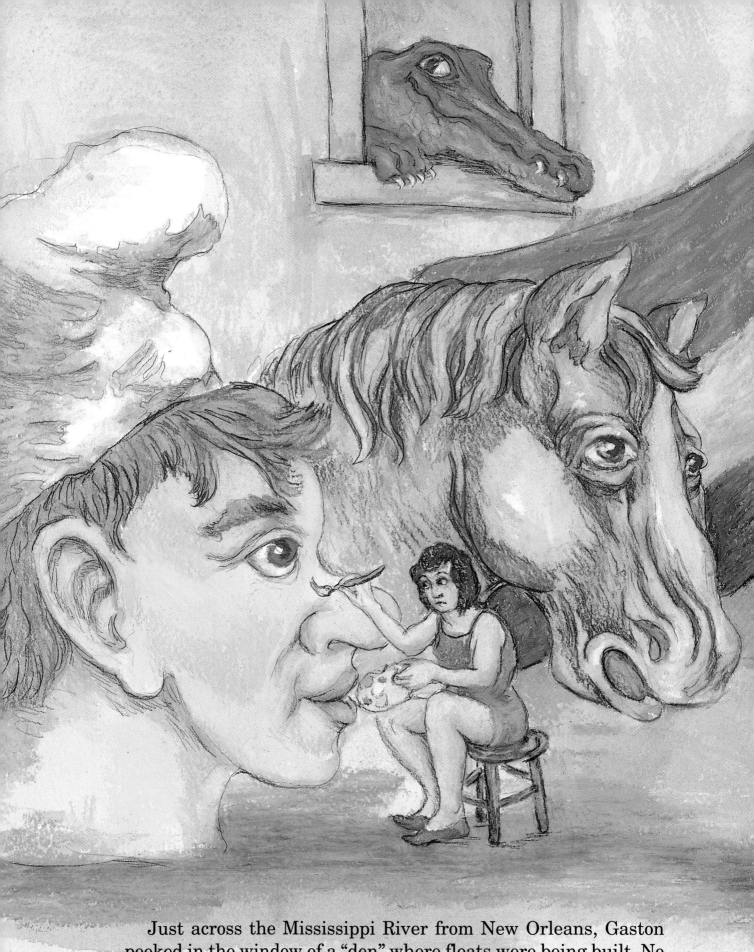

Just across the Mississippi River from New Orleans, Gaston peeked in the window of a "den" where floats were being built. No outsiders were allowed inside.

There were parades every day, reaching a high point on Mardi Gras, or Fat Tuesday, when floats, masked revelers, and Dixieland music filled the streets all day and through the night until midnight.

Gaston liked the black Krewe of Zulu. He rocked to the Dixieland beat and joined his new friends on the float to hand out coconuts to the crowd.

Floats passed one after the other. "Throw me something, Mister!" sounded from the sidelines. Most of the onlookers caught string after string of brightly colored beads. Fewer caught the rarer, shiny doubloons.

The Jefferson City Buzzards, the oldest marching group in the city, were followed by a jazz band. Every member tried to sport the most outlandish costume.

Boeuf Gras, or Fat Beef, the ancient symbol of Mardi Gras, passed. A Boeuf Gras float has been a part of every Mardi Gras since 1959.

Rex's parade, the largest of all the parades, stopped twice en route, once to toast the mayor and once to toast the queen. King Rex and his queen ruled the day with all its festivities.

More parades followed Rex, but few approached the mighty
Rex in terms of lavish display.

The parades and floats continued into the night. The dancing flames from the flambeaus gave many of the floats an eerie, unreal quality.

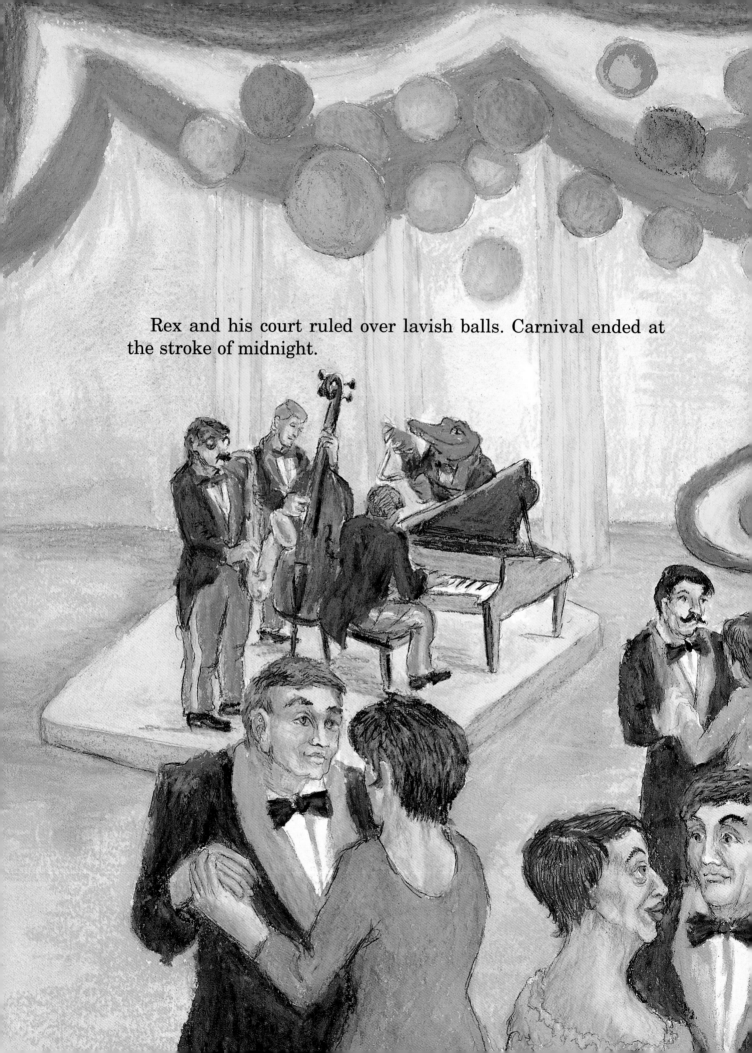

Rex and his court ruled over lavish balls. Carnival ended at
the stroke of midnight.

Mardi Gras was many things, but most of all it was having fun!